CHAPTER 1. WHAT THE HECK?

Invisible disabilities – talk about ruining a totally cool word by plopping it against a word that's utterly depressing. Invisibility has been a fabled superpower since our childhoods. It ranks in the Top 5 Most Wanted Superpowers along with flying, predicting the future, mind reading, and eating nothing but pizza and donuts yet never gaining a single pound.

In the case of an invisible, or hidden, disability, "disability" refers to something assigned to us by a cruel whim of the universe. "Hidden" is a corollary of that whim, the condition that no one can see our disability. They have no idea how we feel. It is left to us to tell them.

But how?

It's like you could write a whole book on the topic. Well *PRESTO*, I did! Here it is.

If you've made it this far, like, you know, *opening* the thing, you surely already know what a hidden disability is. You've got one.

But all the same, I'm going to share with you my definition of *hidden disabilities*, if for no other reason than I worked hard on the thing. See, despite my exhaustive and thorough research, I never found a definition that satisfied me. It's like we're so invisible and perhaps even non-relevant that we can't even get a decent definition. So, I made one up. Because we are *so* relevant.

> ***hidden disabilities*** are conditions that include cognitive difficulties, mental health disorders, learning differences, physical pain, fatigue, or other physical conditions that are not apparent to the

onlooker but significantly impact one's daily activities.

Notice three parts to this definition. The first part covers what a hidden disability might be, from a cognitive impairment to chronic pain. The second part is the "hidden" part: *not apparent to the onlooker*. And finally, the "disability" aspect: the fact that our day-to-day lives are substantially affected. Work. Keeping up the house. Socializing. Pursuing our passions. Taking care of our families, including fur families. Self care. Sex. Flossing. All the things.

One of the great blessings we have in life to help us through difficulties is people. Yes, I'm a fan. But to get help, we need to connect. And to connect, we must be able to communicate.

Let's talk talking.

CHAPTER 2. WHY WE MUST COMMUNICATE

Back to that invisibility superpower. It might be totally awesome to go unseen. Invisibility is the perfect shield against mockery, shaming, judgment, and bumping into the ex in the ice cream section, where invariably you're wearing your most frayed "laundry day" outfit.

But when it comes to disabilities, invisibility can be problematic, in that we totally miss some truly profound benefits to speaking up. The best of which are:

1. Get off our islands.

Living with a hidden disability is living in a lonely place, like being marooned on a desert island, but not even as pretty, and totally devoid of your favorite indulgences you once declared to be your "desert island food" and "desert island song." We're in the place where we feel like no one gets it.

So say something.

I occasionally will post on social media something about my chronic conditions. Usually, it's a statement about the depression which arrives as a symptom of my fibromyalgia. I try my best to describe it—such as how it comes on as suddenly and as naturally and often as inexplicably as a sneeze.

Whatever I'm sharing, every time I do it, whether on social media, at a workshop I present, or with a stranger at Staples, people come out and share back. Nobody's getting cured and nothing's getting solved, but suddenly we're not so alone anymore, and that is definitely something. We've helped each other off our islands.

One time I was waiting on an elevator in a college academic building just after doing a classroom presentation on disabilities. I had dashed out rather quickly after I was done speaking, as the professor had her own lesson to finish up, and I was eager to get on the road ahead of a snowstorm. A student burst out of the classroom and literally ran up to me, crying. Tears of release. All she wanted to say was how grateful she was at not feeling so alone anymore.

Sometimes our disabilities make us feel as if we have so little to give, but this rescue boat off the island is something we *can* give.

2. Prevent misperceptions.

Like I said, I have fibromyalgia. I also have chronic fatigue syndrome, osteoarthritis (in my fingers, toes, and spine), and degenerative disc disease. My least favorite symptoms of all these conditions are the fatigue and cognitive impairment, because they take away time and life.

An annoyance that rides with the cognitive impairment is speech difficulties. When my symptoms are acting up, I may slur, stutter, get words wrong, or just suddenly lose my ability to get words out at all. Being a professional speaker, I can tell you this is *loads* of fun. Actually, it's terrifying.

In each of my programs, I find a way to establish with my audiences that a cognitive impairment may potentially affect my speech. My motivation is to prevent misperceptions. If I do not communicate this, and my symptoms manifest, I set myself up for a slew of inaccurate conclusions such as my being an amateur, or unprepared, or having something other than coffee in my cup.

It does neither me nor my audience any good to annihilate my credibility by failing to communicate about my condition.

Please do the same for yourself. Communicate to others what's going on, so they don't assume the worst about you. Yeah, maybe you have thick skin, and maybe you don't care, but your failing to communicate may prevent you from doing something positive. An example is me, and how my messages of advocacy for our community would fail to transmit if I lost credibility as a speaker.

3. Set expectations.

Nothing ruins a vacation, or a relationship, or even a lasagna like bringing along our silly expectations, yet we all do it just the same, bullheadedly setting ourselves up for disappointment. Other people have expectations of us, and if it's not bad enough having to feel crappy pretty much all the time, we get to go and disappoint the people around us while we're at it.

It'd be way easier if they'd just learn to not have expectations to begin with, but we all know how hard that is. So, as we are often forced to do in all matters life, we need to accept this reality and simply do the next best thing, which is tell people what to expect from us.

How? Well, I'll get to that very soon, because it's the whole point of this book. Right now, I'm covering the "why" first.

4. Give yourself a break.

Speaking of hard things to do, here's one that'll definitely take some courage … but I believe in you!

We become great actors. It's one of the perks of having a disability that's hidden. With a bit of effort, we can keep it hidden. Maybe only for a certain period of time, maybe only on certain days, but it's something most of us can do. It seems easier to just be "normal." It feels like it'll be easier on everyone around us, too. We're doing three huge disservices with our pretending, though. Two of these disservices are covered below in reasons 5 and 6.

The other is just how exhausting it is. When we keep our disabilities hidden instead of accurately communicating—or even passively conveying by simply letting it show—we wear ourselves out in the same way we do in any instance of pretending to be someone we're not. It's just like bluffing in class about a chapter you didn't read, or impressing your high school rivals at the reunion, or cooling your emotions on a date, or curbing your profanity around the in-laws. Pretending wears us out.

It's even worse for those of us with disabilities. Not only are we emotionally and intellectually drained the same way anyone would be, but we are exposing ourselves to that dreaded universal trigger: *stress*.

Stress hits many conditions hard, from depression, to fibromyalgia, to Crohn's. Also, our pretending often involves overly exerting ourselves physically, which, again, can be a devastating trigger for both mental and physical conditions and can even cause serious injury.

I know you hear it all the time. I know you've got stuff to do. I myself have been so guilty of this quite often. A big reason my Splat System exists is to prevent this…. *Don't overdo it.*

Ergo, ease off on the pretending.

5. Incite action with awareness.

This one is very simple but very huge. As long as our disabilities stay hidden, people just won't know. They won't have an inkling what true insomnia feels like. They won't have an understanding of how much diabetes controls your life. They can't fathom how out-of-control rage can be.

And so, no one will do anything about it.

We need awareness because we need research, we need funding, we need the acknowledgement, and we need the cure.

We need prevention.

We need credibility.

We need accessible, affordable, innovative health care ... where medical and mental health professionals, not insurance companies, direct our care.

Again, this is something you—someone who may feel helpless or even useless—can actually *do*. Give. Just, talk about it. Let it show.

6. End the stigma.

This could go under the previous header. As I got listy up there I could have just added in, "We need to end the stigma," but this needs to be talked about a lot more than that, because this needs to be a movement.

I'm talking social movement here.

We live in a realm of humans who so very often expect each other to just keep our "problems" to ourselves. It happens in varying degrees in different subcultures and groups; men, for example are pressured to "man up."

It happens, and it's devastatingly widespread. People just don't want to hear it, or, they "can't be brought down," or they have their own troubles and aren't in the mood for yours, or they deal with things by just ignoring them and think you should, too, because that's supposed to just work for everyone, or they're frustrated about not being able to fix it so they'd just as soon not know, or that's just how they were raised.

Or, that's just what we as a society do.

Then add additional stigma that's specifically assigned to many of the conditions we deal with: bi-polar disorder, depression, and other mental illness; addiction; any condition that makes the fact that we poop more apparent than people are comfortable with....

Judging or shaming someone for a condition we have no control over is simply cruel. OK, fine, sometimes we do actually *cause* our conditions. I'll raise my hand right now and tell you I caused my fibromyalgia—which has its own stigma and punchlines—with my actions. Fibro is known to be activated by a traumatic event, such as a car accident. I caused mine by expansively mismanaging my stress.

There's not a human on this planet over a day old who's never made a mistake. Sometimes those mistakes come with lifelong consequences, but that one action, that one decision, that one moment, does not in any case deserve a whole lifetime of shame.

I don't even like the definition of stigma. If you look it up in the dictionary, the definition includes something like, "a mark of disgrace," as if the person who is the target of a stigma is actually marked, or flawed. But what is stigma really, other than something society just decides in our own brains is unacceptable? There's no literal or figurative mark on someone unless other people place it upon that person like a scarlet letter.

Our best defense against the stigma and the shame is to just talk, like we know there's nothing *wrong* with us. We might be sick people, but we're not bad people. No illness is a moral flaw, and neither is talking about it.

It's not going to happen overnight, and it's definitely not going to be easy, but every time we do communicate about it, in whatever small or big way that's nearly comfortable, we get a little closer to normalizing the conversation. We get a little closer to our disabilities being differences, not marks of disgrace.

CHAPTER 3. THE SPLAT SYSTEM

It's time to talk about the *how*. It's time to talk Splat. This isn't the end-all of how to communicate about hidden disabilities, but it's what I'm so stinking excited to start talking about that I can't wait any longer to share it with you.

This system has a lot to do with the "**moving target**" circumstance. I got this phrase from a good friend of mine who's also a speaker. We always have great conversations about business and often we talk specifically about disabilities, whether teaching about disabilities or just living with them. He has a visible, mobility disability (he was born without legs and uses a wheelchair), and he pointed out a big difference between our situations: that every day, when he wakes up, he knows exactly what his disability is going to be. It never changes, so he can develop coping strategies and accommodations that he can use every day to mask the true impact of his disability on him. My disability, however, is a moving target.

It is true for most of us with hidden disabilities that the severity of our conditions varies. Perhaps it's medication starting and stopping working and changing, or perhaps we're susceptible to triggers, or perhaps we have a progressive illness. Sometimes we have the luxury of knowing how we'll feel the next day. I can look at the weather forecast and take a good guess. Planning a little further ahead is more difficult. I really haven't a clue what my symptoms are going to be next Thursday. I can only do my best to avoid triggers.

The moving target means it's hard to make plans and to keep plans. The moving target makes it hard to establish expectations because the expectations can't be constant. It furthers the strain already placed on our relationships at work, school, home, and the dating scene. It also makes the coveted concept of "routine" a myth in our lives.

The Splat System can't fix all this, but I discovered it can make it a heck of a lot better.

When I first came up with Splat, it didn't have a name. It was just something I used daily, in its most basic way. I was working for a small company as an advertisement and advertorial copywriter. It was a nice gig, and I learned a lot that helped me go on and build my business, but just this simple corporate job was hard. With my fibromyalgia and arthritis, I had a totally unique and definitely more difficult experience doing my daily tasks in my cubicle corner. Sitting is painful. Standing is fatiguing. (I'm lounging on my chaise in my studio as I write this.) Sometimes when I was in a bad flare, I stuttered. It was embarrassing on conference calls, and one time a coworker snapped, "Are you retarded?" when I couldn't get words to follow each other as I explained an ad concept.

I felt like no one understood or appreciated how difficult everything could be for me, how hard I had to work sometimes, how evil it was to always leave donuts and cake in the breakroom.

I don't mean to make my company look cruel or insensitive (except, perhaps that insensitive coworker who called me the R-word). It's not their fault. It's a global problem in our workplaces that there's such a disparaging lack of awareness. As an awareness advocate, it's a personal dream of mine to fix this.

For the time, at that company, one of my greatest coping mechanisms was to have my people. Much to the chagrin of my supervisor, I would often sneak away from my desk and visit the way cooler den of the graphic designers. They were three men, with actual hidden disabilities existing among them as well. We exchanged obscene jokes. We gossiped. We talked about a plethora of nerd stuff. But the greatest way they served my joy and peace at this job was that we talked about my chronic conditions and how they affected me day to day. I could have someone *know*, and that meant the world to me.

Once I got comfortable communicating about my illness, I got a little tired of hearing myself talk about it. It was just so terribly gloomy. I was listing symptoms, and there was always something every day.

Then one day I walked in and declared this:

Every single day I feel like I've been run over by

something. That's just a given, and that's how it'll be forever. But it's by a different vehicle on different days.

From then on, I no longer walked in and told them how tired I was or how foggy my brain was, or how much my hands hurt. I could simply say, "moped," or "pickup truck," or "freight train." And they got it.

It was awesome!

I could be straight-forward, light-hearted, and non-whiney, and still *leave my island.*

The Splat System has now evolved way past its original use. For example, I can use it to finally have and keep an actual routine, despite my varying state of wellness. But first things first. You need to know…

— *The Splat Scale* —

moped

My symptoms are *always* there, but today they're pretty chill!

Eurocar

My symptoms are holding me back a little, but I can do more today than usual.

sedan

Just a standard day with this illness. I don't feel well, but I can do the things.

pickup truck

I can almost get by like a normal person today, but everything is a huge struggle and I want my mommy.

tractor trailer

Everything mean they ever said about this disease is true. I feel absolutely awful. If it's critically important, I'll do it. The rest of life will have to wait.

freight train

All of my symptoms are at their worst. I'm totally miserable, and I couldn't keep my "invisible" illness invisible if I tried. If you need me, I'll be in my bed, and, well, just *don't* need me.

asteroid

Zombies are more alive than I am.

There you have it. Now, let's talk about all the ways we can use this, besides chatting with the coworkers you share fart jokes with.

CHAPTER 4. GOOD GRIEF

I know I said we were going to talk about using the Splat System, but please grant me this one digression first. It's important.

About a year and a half after I got my fibro, and several months after my diagnosis, I had a blubbering breakdown at a friend's house. The breakdown showed up with zero warning and zero cause (except yes, if I'm going to be totally honest, there *was* some wine involved).

I sank into despair. All of the ramifications and realities of fibromyalgia stormed through my core, and over and over I was saying, "I'm going to have this forever. It's not OK."

It wasn't much different than when I didn't cry over my grandpa's death until I was sitting through the funeral service; days of suppression exploded out in ugly sobs.

I'd had no idea that I needed to grieve.

But we do need to grieve. Whether we were born with something or have been recently diagnosed—or are in that purgatory of "undiagnosed"—there is most definitely a huge loss. There are things we will never be able to do. Maybe we used to be able to do them, and they've been taken away forever. I can never run a 5K again and it crushes me. Maybe there are things you've never gotten to experience and never will, but you know they exist, because all the "normals" out there are doing them every day, right in front of you. These things might include the ability to feel calm.

I highly recommend grieving. Get yourself through a process of grief, but don't put *too* much pressure on "acceptance." While I accept my conditions, they'll never be OK. What I mean is ... it's similar to when I had braces on my teeth; even after two years, the day I had them taken off they *still* didn't feel OK in my mouth. My chronic fatigue and chronic pain will never, ever, ever feel OK. I'll always know that there's a different, better way that I should feel. However, I accept that this is how it's going to be for the rest of my life. It's up to me to make the very best of it, just as it is for anyone.

Whatever it looks like for you, because grief is different for everyone just as no two cases of your chronic condition are alike, please grieve. Otherwise, your ugly crying might obliterate a perfectly good Saturday when all your friends want to do is eat some bacon cheddar ranch tater tots and watch *Game of Thrones*.

CHAPTER 5. COMMUNICATING WITH OURSELVES

Chronic illness, whether mental, cognitive, physical, or a combination of these, demands we have conversations with ourselves daily. I made sure I went over grief prior to this chapter because even when you're done grieving, you're still never done.

Wait, what?

There are the daily losses. You know what yours are.

Splat is about to totally change some of these losses for you, though. Are you ready to have the concept of routine back, no matter what?

Here's the wonderful simple way to do it.

Every day, you must be the first person you tell what Splat vehicle weight you're at. I call it my "Splatus," and I establish mine between coffees one and two. It's lovely because, same as I did with my coworkers, I can shield myself from having to hear all about my exact symptoms all day. I'll just think, wow, I'm more tired than usual, my gut is a wreck, and I've got that pre-storm shoulder ache that's usually not there. After my initial assessment of symptoms, the rest of the day I simply remind myself that it's a pickup truck day.

Ahead of time, I've established what I'm going to do each day depending on what vehicle I'm at. I have written down, in a grid sketched in my notebook, expectations of myself in different categories depending on what weight I'm at. One column is "Word Studio" (my name for my home office). There are three boxes under that heading. One is next to "moped, Eurocar, sedan" (M-E-S), one is next to "pickup truck, tractor trailer" (P-T), and the other next to "freight train, asteroid" (F-A). In the M-E-S box, I have "7 hours," the amount of time I expect to work in my studio if I'm at that level. Next to P-T is "5 hours." Next to F-A is "essential calls and emails only."

I have another column for what my workouts are going to be per level. Another column is how long my dog's walks are going to be.

Another is "self-care." While in other columns I do less and less the heavier a vehicle is, this is one where I do more and more the heavier it is. At F-A, for example, I bust out the aromatherapy and allow myself Chinese takeout.

There's a different kind of self-care column, too. This one is about personal grooming. If I'm at anything better than freight train, I need to get a shower and put on a little makeup. ***Figure 1*** is a variation of my personal daily expectations table, called the **Impact Map**.

Figure 1: Impact Map

	WORK	EXERCISE	PET CARE	APPEARANCE	SELF-CARE
MOPED EUROCAR SEDAN	7 hours in office	3 sets of 10 + yoga	45 minutes of walking	shower & makeup	just the usual dog cuddles
P. TRUCK T. TRAILER	5 hours in office	2 sets of 10	30 minutes of walking	shower & makeup	take breaks or a nap
F. TRAIN ASTEROID	essential calls & emails only	nope	empties only	who cares?	aromatherapy & say yes to soup offers

This system changed my life. While I've got a whole bunch of other stuff to give you in this book, the Impact Map is one of the biggest reasons this book had to happen.

At last, I can keep a routine. What I do each day still varies, but these variations don't mean I'm straying from an overall plan. I've established what will happen each day depending on how I feel, and I stick with it. I no longer wrestle with motivating myself. I just assess how I feel after that first coffee and look in my little book and follow what it says. I no longer feel guilty about what doesn't get done. I just get done what I'm supposed to that day and celebrate the accomplishment. I can give myself a break, a day off, but on the flip side, I can no longer use my conditions as excuses.

I'll reiterate because it's so absolutely wonderful:

> *It eliminates guilt. It eliminates excuses. It resurrects your concept of routine.*

Right now—yes this exact moment—draw your own Impact Map. If you like, go to www.TalkingSplat.com and download the one I made for you to fill out.

Tips to make it work:

1. Numbers matter.

It's essential your daily expectations are quantifiable so you're not putting yourself on the spot to make judgments in the moment and setting yourself up for guilt or failure. That pretty much defeats the purpose. So rather than "spend some time crocheting," write, "spend one hour crocheting." Get it?

2. Start out of order.

Start in the P-T row and write in what you know you can do no matter what.

Add extra stuff in the M-E-S row. Accomplishing more than usual will give you peace about the F-A days when you accomplish less.

Finally, in the F-A row, write in only what absolutely must get done to prevent your world from burning down.

3. Keep it sacred.

This is a written contract with yourself. It's not negotiable. Make sure you only require of yourself what you're actually willing to do and then stick with it.

4. Include specific daily tasks.

Try writing a new one each week and add your specific daily chores and errands in. It'll double as your to-do list, and you'll get it all done. Just make sure those essential chores and errands are in both the M-E-S and P-T rows.

While you're at it, include "snow days" (northerners like me remember this from grade school), or built-in blocks of time to do a workout or chore you may have missed another day due to a freight train or asteroid. ***Figure 2*** is an example, including makeup times.

Figure 2: Daily Impact Map

	MON.	TUE.	WED.	THU.	FRI.	SAT.	SUN.
	work: 7 hours gym: 3x10, yoga dog: 45 mins. shower & makeup	work: 7 hours gym: 3x10, yoga dog: 45 mins. shower & makeup	work: 7 hours dog: 45 mins. dust, sweep, vacuum shower & makeup	work: 7 hours gym: 3x10, yoga dog: 45 mins. trash, plants shower & makeup	work: 7 hours gym: 3x10, yoga dog: 45 mins. shower & makeup	work: 3 hours dog: 45 mins. cleaning project sweep vacuum m/u gym m/u shower & makeup	dog: 45 mins. shower & makeup
	work: 5 hours gym: 2x10 dog: 30 mins. shower & makeup	work: 5 hours gym: 2x10 dog: 30 mins. shower & makeup	work: 5 hours sweep & vacuum dog: 30 mins. shower & makeup	work: 5 hours gym: 2x10 dog: 30 mins. trash shower & makeup	work: 5 hours gym: 2x10 dog: 30 mins. shower & makeup	dog: 30 mins. cleaning project sweep vacuum m/u gym m/u shower & makeup	dog: 30 mins. shower & makeup
	essential calls & emails dog: empties	essential calls & emails dog: empties	essential calls & emails dog: empties	essential calls & emails dog: empties trash	essential calls & emails dog: empties	dog: empties	dog: empties

m/u = "makeup" if missed on prior day

5. Use Splat to make plans.

We get tired of having to cancel plans because of unexpected tractor trailer days. Try making plans with the Impact Map mindset and see if you can prevent cancellations.

I recently planned a girls' day with a good friend who is understanding of my conditions. We chose a date in the future and agreed that if I am at M-E-S on that day, we'll go thrift store shopping then grab dinner. If I am at P-T, we'll get takeout and do a movie night. If I am at F-A, we've got to limit it to one movie and soup and we'll be piling on my bed.

6. Be honest with yourself.

Don't rank yourself a heavier vehicle just because you don't feel like doing something that day.

Likewise, don't rank yourself a lighter vehicle just because you want to feel more productive. Sticking with the Impact Map *is* productive, and taking care of yourself with mindfulness and kindness is super important. Remember, part of why you must communicate with yourself is so that you don't overdo it.

7. Be willing to change your scale.

I once noticed I hadn't had a moped day in six months, so I decided it was time to change what I thought a moped day was. Your scale may change seasonally.

8. Try a signal.

For you, as well for those in your Splat circle, keep an indicator in your space that says where you're at each day. Maybe a sticky note in your cubicle. I made myself a bracelet with color-coded, interchangeable pendants (you can get your own at www.SplattieStore.com if you like) so I can remind myself where I'm at and what my responsibilities are. It's also a reminder that I have a condition and I can't go along kidding myself that I don't; that only makes things worse.

Now, when I go on vacation, I do leave the bracelet home and absolutely do whatever I want, but I do it with the understanding and compromise that there will be consequences. It surely is nice, though, to take the little break from disease, and my signal allows me to do this by being something visual in my space that I can remove. This isn't something I recommend for everyone, but it may be safe and viable for you depending on your condition.

9. Limit it to six days a week.

I have spiritual reasons for taking a **day of rest**, but I've noticed the necessity and benefits of this day transcend religion. We just need a break. We can never take a break from our diseases, but we can take one day a week to ignore our Splat level and just chill no matter what.

It's a fine way to take care of ourselves and enjoy a sense of freedom that can be too rare. Consider doing something extra special for yourself this day as a reward for sticking with your Impact Map all week. Like that binge-watch-a-thon you've been resisting like a champ.

10. You don't have to do this alone.

Talk through your choices with your partner or your bestie. Recruit someone to help hold you accountable. Team up with a pal with a hidden disability and make your Impact Maps together and check in with each other regularly.

You can even make a special "what to do" column for your partner, parent, or bestie that informs them what your needs are from them based on what your Splatus is.

Did you do it yet? No? Not feeling ready? Well let me tell you this, then….

When I was a sophomore in college, I did something extremely terrifying. I did a five-minute stand-up comedy routine at an open mic night. It ended up becoming my first career when I graduated. I did hundreds of shows before I turned twenty-five, and those experiences have everything to do with everything I am today. Yet, it almost never happened.

If it weren't for twelve words my friend Bill said to me, my life would have taken a totally different course. I'll give you the short version with the important part (the full kismetic tale is going in a totally different book).

My friend Bill is a brilliant and hilarious magician, and he knew I had interest in trying stand-up comedy someday. When a new comedy club was about to open and they hired Bill to emcee the shows the first week, he called me and told me about the open mic night. He told me I needed to come perform.

What do you think I said?

No! In every way possible. I came up with every reason I could think of to not get onstage, and I was a creative writing student, so the list was profound.

That's when he said it.

" if you don't do it now, you're never going to do it."

I couldn't argue with that. Who can? He was right.

I did do it, and it gave me everything, not the least of which is those twelve words that I've lived by ever since. I even added a corollary, which is, "There's never a *right* time, but there is a *good* time."

Whatever your excuses are, they're not going away, or if they do, new ones will be right there to take their place. You might as well just get on with it.

Your Impact Map is not written in stone. You can change it any time. And there's no professor who's going to grade your work. Just get something on paper and start following it.

If you don't do it now, you're never going to do it.

CHAPTER 6. SPLAT ON THE JOB

When I do trainings, questions relating to disability at work often come up in the Q&A time. The moving target plus expectations is a big issue. Getting coworkers and supervisors to be understanding and accommodating is another big issue. I experienced such difficulties myself, and when attendees ask these questions, I feel like my answers fall short.

I have the great privilege of now being self-employed, but I remember too well what it was like to deal with my disabilities at a workplace. You recall it's how the Splat System came about.

My impossible dream is to be able to present my invisible disabilities awareness program at every single workplace in the whole world. Mere awareness would make such a difference for people with hidden disabilities at work. I'm doing my very best, but remember you too can further the cause by communicating and normalizing disability.

I know, it's still easier said than done.

Not all bosses are understanding. Not all coworkers are nice. I can't solve this for you. I wish I could.

The best I can offer is for you to know your rights granted by the Americans with Disabilities Act. Use whatever internal resources are available to you, such as human resources or an employee assistance program. Make allies so you can leave your island. Use the Splat System.

If you choose to display your Splatus each day, don't place actual expectations on anyone but yourself. To others, it should be a gentle helpful hint, not a burden to force empathy, and not a victim poster. We all need to keep Splat reverent and positive.

Fit your daily tasks into your Impact Map and make sure the work you need to do is on the P-T line. Then, when you're at M-E-S, you'll be a rock star, and when you're at F-A, you'll hopefully be forgiven. The best-case scenario is for you to explain your moving target situation to your supervisor and coworkers and even get your supervisor to collaborate with you on creating your workplace Impact Map. Make it very clear that you'll perform up to expectations at P-T and exceed expectations at M-E-S to make up for the F-A days. Show your value.

If you cannot perform your job to expectations on a P-T day, then use your available resources and allies and see what changes might be available to you. You've got to be reasonable with yourself and not set yourself up for failure.

Another one of my mottos is this:

> *Don't try to find your perfect solution; look at the solutions that actually exist and choose the best one.*

CHAPTER 7. SECRETS FROM THE STAGE

You want to be heard. You probably understand that you *need* to be heard. But how? You can't force people to listen. You can't make them change their minds.

Sometimes, you actually can. I know some proven tricks to doing so that have been tried and tested in an unexpected place.

This isn't mind control; it's persuasion meets performance. I've been around show business for more than 20 years, many of which have been spent touring as a stand-up comedian. I've also studied, taught, and performed theatre, both improvised and scripted. Add on to that my four years' work in persuasive performance as a classroom teacher and my current gig as a professional speaker. Plus, my work on the printed page as an ad copywriter is of note in this mix.

From all my time on all these "stages," I've picked up some brilliant strategies for communication. I won't guarantee the miracle that you'll suddenly be widely acknowledged and understood, but if you embody these ideas and fully use the ones you feel comfortable with, of course it'll make a big difference in your being heard.

Try these tricks to communicate about your hidden disability, for all the reasons I shared in Chapter 1. But also, try them in all the things that matter in your life, all those times when you've got something important to say.

1. Know your objective.

This is theatre 101. Literally. Objective, in this case, is what you want. And it's going to drive you. Think about going for a walk just to take a stroll. Then think about walking to a specific place with a specific task. Your stride is different, isn't it? Because with the latter, you have a purpose, a destination, an objective.

If that analogy doesn't work for you, think jigsaw puzzles. You use that picture on the box lid, don't you? They're way harder if you don't. Everything is way harder if you don't know where you're going.

Whether in speaking or writing, have an objective. Know the outcome you want. Otherwise, you're rambling.

Some pointers:

A) State your objective in your mind as "I want ____________." Always include "I want" and fill in the blank with as few words as possible. Be specific. It's stronger that way.

B) When an actor dissects a script, he or she comes up with a multitude of objectives, and they nest within each other. Each moment has an objective. Those objectives fit within a larger objective of a scene. Each objective of a scene fits within a larger objective of the act, which henceforth fit into the largest objective, the "**superobjective**." The superobjective drives the whole play (or movie, or book … a story is a story).

What do you want in a moment? Does it fit into what you want for your day, and does it fit into what you want out of life right now? Knowing this full range of your personal objectives will pack power in your statements and actions.

C) Objectives can be even stronger when you attach them to another person. Instead of "I want ____________," try "I want (*so-and-so*) to ____________."

By the way, I can't help but add that *objective* isn't limited to the context of communication. Objective is a *life* thing. So while we're here, I strongly encourage you to figure out that one thing you want more than anything in the world right now. Know it and hold it close. Treasure it and let it drive you. Trust me. I did this for the first time in a theatre class exercise in college and it drove me right out of an abusive relationship. I had to pick one word to sum up what I wanted most in the world, and the word I picked was "freedom." My precious word led me, I got it, and I've kept it.

You can go even further and pick an objective for each day when you assess your Splat level. Even write it down on your Impact Map, because writing stuff down amplifies its power.

The more you know your objectives, the better a head start you'll have when it does come time to be heard, and the more authentic you'll be.

Remember, you're not your disability or disease. You're you, with your dreams and goals. Some days you'll just want to get through the day, but try as much as you're able to put yourself above your disease when you choose your objectives.

2. Be likeable.

There's a trick in screenwriting where in the first five minutes or so, you include a quick scene for the sole purpose of endearing the main character to the audience. It could be picking up a stuffed animal that a child dropped and returning it. Maybe it's an empathy moment, such as the hero being bullied and injured. Whatever it is, it's usually there. Look for it the next time you watch a movie.

I went through a phase as a comedian where I wore my long, strawberry blonde hair in a ponytail tucked away in a baseball cap. It made me more androgynous and therefore less susceptible to any stereotypical prejudices against female comedians. It was one strategy in my overall objective to make the audience like me, so they'd laugh at my jokes.

You might have gone to a comedy show where a comedian just comes across as a complete jerk and there's nothing funny about it.

It's so much easier to be respected and heard if you're likeable. Think about it. Do you listen when someone is yelling at you in anger?

One of the fallback strategies for comedians to be likeable is self-deprecation. When you make people feel better about themselves—so, in this case, better than you—they like you. This is why comedians make fun of people, so that the audience can feel superior and be more prone to laugh.

I'm not keen on bullying, though.

The easiest, kindest way to make someone feel better about themselves is to pay them a genuine compliment.

The easiest way to be likeable is kindness.

When you're comfortable doing so, show your authentic vulnerability and appeal to the kindness in others. It may not always feel like it, but kindness is just as real in them as it is in you.

3. Remove barriers.

There's a very simple, yet very impactful mistake that a lot of aspiring comedians make at their first open mic nights. They take the microphone out of the mic stand but leave the stand just sitting there in front of them. It's a slender pole that can hardly obscure a zipper, but it's a barrier. It's a literal thing coming between the comic and his or her audience.

When you're trying to communicate with someone, is there something between you? It may be something physical and big, like a desk. Maybe it's subtle, like the notebook you're clutching to your chest. It could be a vast space, much like when a shy comedian hugs the back wall of the stage instead of coming forward to be more within the audience.

It could be a figurative or symbolic barrier. This may be harder to remove, but certainly try to clear up any prejudices, misconceptions, grudges, or resentments that come between you and whomever you're communicating with.

4. Know your audience.

I can't do the same show in a theatre in Wisconsin as I'd do in a dive bar near a military base in Alabama, or in a bowling alley in Nebraska. These different venues draw different audiences, and I have to tailor my content accordingly. I had to work clean when I played Charleston, but Carbondale wanted it a bit more in the gutter.

When you're applying for a job, create different versions of your resume for each place you're applying to. Pull out the experience and skills that matter most to each one.

You're still you, but you're tailoring your personal content to whom you're speaking. Who are they, what do they want to hear, and how do they want to hear it?

5. Believe in what you're selling.

So much of life is sales. You have something you want to give, and you need someone to want to have it. You're selling your lasagna to your wife. You're selling bedtime to your kids. You're selling the green beans diet to your dog. You're selling a new widget design to your boss. You're selling your joke to your father-in-law. You're selling your sociology paper to your professor, and within it you're selling your thesis statement. You're selling lawn boundaries to your neighbors and their children and their dog.

I was a waitress at a brewpub that had great beer and incredible food, especially the burgers and stromboli. Customers often took my recommendations happily and I earned great tips. Then the restaurant started to have issues with staffing, and these issues translated to long cook times and substandard food. I didn't believe in the burgers and 'bolis anymore and hence had a terrible time selling them. I quit because I wasn't making the money I once did and I was frustrated serving crap food to good people.

Likewise, I've gone on hiatuses from the stage, sometimes lasting over a year. People would ask me if I was ever going to perform again, and my answer was always yes ... when I write new material. I'd outgrown and grown tired of my old jokes and didn't believe in them anymore. Comedy is definitely sales, and when you don't believe in the jokes you're selling, they're not funny.

Whatever it is you're trying to communicate, especially when you need a certain reaction from someone, you must truly believe in it. If not, you're just going through the motions and they're not apt to buy it (I'll wager it doesn't even fit with your superobjective).

6. Practice past fear.

Audiences can tell when a performer is scared, and they buck that act off like a horse flinging a nervous passenger. Students will rebel against the uncertain substitute teacher. If you're trying to present an idea, and you're wriggling with nerves, your fear is going to be louder than your message.

Overcoming fear is a tall order, especially if your hidden disability includes anxiety.

Let me tell you a couple things that help me in case they might help you.

First, I've figured out there are only three types of fear that hold us back from saying or doing things:

> A) The fear of embarrassment, being judged, or anything having to do with what other people think
>
> B) The fear of making a mistake or failing, or anything having to do with not being able to do something
>
> C) The fear of harm—to yourself or others, whether physical or emotional

This third/"C" fear is a good fear. It keeps us safe. If the fear of causing harm ever stops you from doing something, good. Let it. It's doing its job.

As for fearing embarrassment and fearing failure, we've all experienced embarrassment and failure, and we're still here. We survived it. So why would you let something you've already proven to yourself that you can survive stop you from reaching your objective? I don't.

We already have too many obstacles. Don't let fear become another one. In truth, fear is often nothing more than an excuse.

I know, once again, I easily say something that's super hard to do, so here's my second discovery.

Overcoming the detriments of fear takes practice. It's just like going to the gym. The more you show up, the more exercises you do, the heavier the weights you lift, the more reps, the stronger you get. Yes, you have to build up to it.

For my first time traveling overseas alone, I went to England because they speak English. The next time, I did something more challenging and went to Germany, but I do know a little German. Then I went to Italy knowing barely any Italian but comfortable now in Europe and more than comfortable with pizza and gelato. I've now been to 19 countries, including Brazil, where I traveled 12 hours by careening bus to a remote little town in the Minas Gerais state.

Practice. It's OK to start with the little pink weights. Go eat out alone. Wear that weird outfit. Then add heavier weights. Build up your courage muscles. Stick with it and you might surprise yourself. Just please don't practice on "C"-fear things!

7. Make every word count.

Actors have the luxury of scripts, and most plays that are produced have reasonably good ones. To be heard, actors need only be brave and sell.

Many comedians write out, memorize, and hone our material. Newbies often make a certain mistake with their words that should be avoided in general conversation, professional meetings, and written correspondence.

The mistake is being verbose. You'll make a stronger point if you stay on topic and say only what you need to prove your point. Specificity includes using real concrete details and actions and sparing your personal opinions.

I once reported being sexually harassed at work and the man got fired. My report didn't include my emotions and opinions on the matter or on the man himself, nor was there even a request for him to be fired. I simply wrote down what he said verbatim then read these notes to my supervisor, and just the facts got me heard and got him removed from my space.

You already know to avoid filler words like "um" and "uh." Some comedians use profanity as filler words, cussing like it's commas. Totally amateur, cheap, and even offensive. Nearly as bad is adding in "like," "seems like," or "kinda." Say it like you mean it! If something *seems like* it's too hot to eat, I'm not inclined to believe you. Commit. Sell.

My personal pet peeve is "I feel like." I worked with a guy who, every time he stated an opinion, said it with "I feel like…" Dude, I know it's how *you* feel. You're the one saying it.

I feel like I made my point.

One more thing here: Don't fear the pause. Watch a good actor or comedian perform. There are moments of silence in there, and those moments do a lot of work. They're scary, yes, but use your new courage muscles and give it a try.

8. Prepare for hecklers.

I'm going to tell you a secret about improv and ad-libbing in comedy: It's usually not made up on the spot. That comedian you like who picks on the crowd and always asks, "What's your name? Where do you work?" He's already met dozens or hundreds of dentists and is already prepared with a well-honed, seemingly spontaneous response.

Pros stand ready to react to hecklers with stock lines such as, "I don't come down to where you work and knock the French fries out of your hands, do I?" or "I remember when I had my first beer" or "There's a reason the lights are pointing at me," or they have their own that they've come up with over the years and use frequently and successfully.

You know those times when you get in a confrontation with someone and hours or days later you think of the perfect thing to say? I say make like a comedian and have your "ad libs" ready to go ahead of time. What are the common insensitive things people say?

- *You didn't seem to have a problem doing that yesterday.*

- *Have you actually been diagnosed with that?*

- *Everyone has something.*

These are just three examples. I'll go no further down that path of negativity. You know what they are, and you know what the ones specific to your condition are. Do some brainstorming. Come up with your responses and keep them in your mental bag of tricks.

Personal favor to me, though…. Remember you are an advocate for awareness for us all. While it may seem satisfying in the moment to be cleverly mean to someone being insensitive, it'll be harder for your very important message to be heard if you're not likeable. Snark is fun. Meanness kills your opportunity to teach. Craft your witty responses within your objective and shoehorn in some kindness where you can.

Here's one I have:

> **Insensitive person:** *Did a doctor tell you you have that?*
>
> **Me:** *Yes, but it did take a year to diagnosis. It's really hard to diagnose, which is why we struggle with credibility, but that's getting better.*

I like my response because giving a personal detail about my diagnostic process makes it real and gives me believability. I also slide in a teaching moment when I say credibility is hard, while at the same time implying I get why she might be questioning me. I didn't call her an idiot, so she's more apt to listen.

9. Don't apologize.

I learned this lesson offstage, and I learned it the hard way. After a really difficult show, I was hanging out in the venue chatting with another comedian, talking about how awful I did and how much the crowd hated me (hundreds of people *literally turned around* and ignored me before I even grabbed the microphone!). I did all this within earshot of the staff.

They were likely so busy they didn't even notice how terribly my show went, but now they knew for sure. When they sent their report to the booking agency, who booked this and many other clubs I worked, they said I was awful. I got fired from the agency and lost a lot of work over it.

If you say you did something wrong, people will believe you, and chances are, you're probably just being hard on yourself. Credibility is hard enough without you notching it away on your own. So if you're going to speak openly about failures, or use the words "I'm sorry," make sure you actually *need* to.

10. Be in love.

Remember how excited I was to share the Splat System with you? Well I'm nearly as excited about sharing this. See, I had a big frustration when I first started in stand-up comedy. Everyone was saying, "Work on your stage presence." How? Besides just doing it? They made it sound like there was something I could suddenly do tomorrow that'll make me way better than I was tonight.

The elusive *stage presence.*

I also thought maybe it's something you either have or you don't. That it's impossible to "work on."

Then I went to a play and discovered something monumental. The play was *The Rainmaker*, and while it was regional theatre, David Keith, a movie star originally from the area, had the lead role. Just not the night I was there. I happened to buy a ticket for his day off, and his understudy, a local professor, led the performance.

What at first was a disappointment turned out to have a serious impact on the rest of my life. I was entranced by this understudy actor. He had such a glow and a presence onstage that it was seemingly divine. I'd seen this level of talent, this very particular "glow," a few times before. When I saw Boots Randolph live, playing his sax, it was so there. I've seen it more since.

One other place I've seen it, that I immediately called to mind when I watched that play, was not on any stage. I recognized it as the exact glow that the two most in-love people I've ever seen have when they are around each other.

That's what I saw in that actor's performance. He was in love. In love with the stage, the play, his audience. *That* is stage presence.

I told you everything is sales, that you have to believe in what you're selling. I told you kindness matters and you want to be likeable. With and beyond it all, if you're saying or doing something you want heard, felt, or learned, *love it.* Find in or use in your performance something that you are overflowing with passion about, and no one will be able to look away.

CHAPTER 8. SELF-CARE TOOLBOX

I'm going to veer now from the overall topic of communication and give you just a few more things. I know what you're going through is hard. Hidden disabilities suck. Aside from figuring out ways to communicate about what I'm going through, and aside from using the Impact Map, I've got other ways I manage my own hidden disability that I want to share.

When I teach people how to share an idea about self-care, I teach to present them as just that: an idea. Don't present it as a miracle or a cure, don't expect what works for you will work for them, don't pressure them to do it, and likewise be mindful that they may not have the comfort level, access, or money to do it.

That's how I'm presenting these ideas to you. They often help me, and I hope maybe they can help you too, but if you don't dig them, it won't hurt my feelings.

1. Find your people.

Make sure that, wherever you are, you can get off your island if you need to. Whether you find others going through something like you are, or just kind compassionate people, see if you can make sure you've got a plant in all your worlds. Have someone at work you can talk to about your illness without judgment. Figure out what relatives you can bond with at the holiday events. Even find another parent at your son's soccer games. Knowing who you can talk to about anything is super helpful.

2. Get lost.

No, I don't mean it like *that*. What I mean is.... You know those things you do that you get so caught up in that time flies by and you forget about the world? For me, it's my sudoku app on my phone, or organizing a closet, or watching all my Jane Austen movies (including Bridget Jones by association) for the millionth time. Whatever they are for you, keep track of them, and go there and do that when you need to step away from your own crap for a little while.

3. Solve the symptoms.

You may have renovated a house or written a dissertation and realized that huge overwhelming projects are much more doable when you look away from the big intimidating picture and take them on one manageable piece at a time. That's how I deal with my hidden disabilities.

It's totally overwhelming to look at it all together and try to do something about it: fibromyalgia, chronic fatigue syndrome, osteoarthritis, and degenerative disc disease. Jeez, I had to rest after just typing that list. Never mind the infinite symptoms attached.

I've picked out my grievances one at a time and I look at them independently to see what I can do about it. My irritable bowel syndrome (IBS), for example: I went on a low carb diet and my intestines are much happier now. Back when I had my corporate job, showering early in the morning wiped me out. I couldn't *solve* that necessarily, but I could start showering at night, so I did. I happily traded bathing brownouts for bad hair days.

List your specific symptoms, starting with your least favorite, and see what you can do to help each, one at a time.

Remember, as I said before: Don't try to have your ideal solution. Just look at the solutions available and pick the best one.

4. Communicate.

Oh look! I'm back on topic! And yes, I've already shared a ton about communication, particularly the *why* and the *how*, but I'd like to add a bit on the *what*. You know all those people of yours? The ones who care and want to help? First, you should let them know what vehicle you've been run over by today. Then, if it's a tractor trailer truck, a freight train, or an asteroid, how about letting them know how they can help?

We sometimes get frustrated when it seems like no one cares, but often it's because they don't know that they need to care, and they especially don't know how to show it. Romantic partners and parents especially really want to help and often need our help in knowing just what to do.

People aren't mind readers, so tell them. What makes you feel better? What kind of soup do you want Mom to bring over? Don't feel like you're a whiner or a bother. They love you and hate feeling helpless all the time. They'll feel so good, being able to actually *do* something for you, that really *you* are doing *them* a favor!

Maybe even make this a column on your Impact Map: "What to ask for."

5. Remember the cycle.

I really hope you're having a good day today. If you are, I'm sure you remember worse days. They passed. If you're having a bad day, I'm so sorry. Please hold on to knowledge of the cycle and that it will pass, just as it has before.

I mentioned my depression. I call mine The Darkness. When fall into it, I use my awareness of the "cycle" in my special trick to get out of it.

Depression is a horrific monster that is different for everyone, and you may be someone who needs a doctor and/or medication for yours, just as I recently became a person who needs a doctor and some wonderful little pills for my IBS. This trick for depression is by no means a cure, and it's not a viable strategy for everyone, but it works great for me.

As I know full well that it will pass, I don't pressure myself to feel better. I don't shame myself for being sad. I just dig in. But there are terms to this agreement. I have an allowance. Three days. For three days I'm allowed to feel totally and utterly sorry for myself. I'll break my diet and order Chinese food, and then before it's all gone, I'll order more Chinese food, because who can ever finish Chinese anyway? I'll cry. I'll call my mom crying. I'll call my out-of-state besties, crying. I'll watch every chick flick I own then go to Target and buy more chick flicks … and Legos.

What inevitably happens is by the end of day two, I'm so tired of feeling sorry for myself that I just snap out of it altogether. All that remains is the bloating.

6. Celebrate your wins.

Bear with me here, because I need to discuss soccer, lawnmowing, and golf.

Did you ever in your life play a sport? Did you as an individual or did your team lose more than you won? That was the case with my high school soccer team. We were awful. We were a joke in our division.

I decided then that it was better to be on a losing team than a winning team.

Think about it. When you're used to losing, losing is no big deal, and winning is the most awesomest thing ever! Contrarily, when you're used to winning, winning is no big deal and losing is devastating.

Which range of emotions would you rather feel?

I thought about this dichotomy specifically a couple of summers ago when I had to mow my lawn. It was a Saturday morning, and I woke up feeling like someone squoze my head all night. I was super dizzy tired. My hands hurt. Definite tractor trailer day.

I have what I call a ten-minute lawn, which means it only takes ten minutes to mow. To most people, that's no big deal. To me, on that Saturday, it was impossible.

But it had to be done, so I rolled out of bed, put on pants, and spent the ten miserable minutes mowing my lawn.

When I was done, I felt like I'd achieved the impossible. I felt like a superhero. I don't care if my lawn is no big deal to everyone else. That day, I won, and it was the awesomest thing ever.

Life isn't fair. When you've got a hidden disability, it's downright crappy a lot of the time. I can only hope that as you read this, you're at a time in your life when you win more than you lose … and that it stays that way. If so, keep celebrating those wins. Every one. Don't take them for granted. And try not to be so hard on yourself when you lose. It happens to us all.

More likely, you feel like you're on that losing team, and I'm so sorry this is what life has dealt you. Celebrate your wins. All of them. I don't care if it's something that doesn't mean a thing to anyone else. If it's a big deal to you, then it's a big deal. Celebrate.

Or, what if you could just win *all the time*? If you're ready and willing to celebrate a megaton of wins, I'll tell you how. It has to do with golf.

When I worked at a golf course, it was common for me to ask, "How did you play today?" when a golfer finished his round and bellied up to my bar.

One day, a golfer replied, "Great! How did *you* play today?"

"I've been working all day!" I replied.

He just smiled and said, "I know! How did you play today?"

First of all, try that. Try substituting the word "play" for "work" any chance you get. It'll give you a much cooler mindset. I so much prefer to *play* in my Word Studio than *work*.

The bigger point is this: Looking back to my days of soccer, I don't think it was the fact that I was used to losing that made losing OK.

I was never a naturally talented athlete. When I was in second grade, I was one of only two kids in my class who had to wear the stinky foam egg floaty thing on my back when we did gym class at the pool. As a soccer player, I was baffled at all the fancy footwork the actual talented players could do. I had to opt for more reckless tactics which earned me the nickname, *Kamikaze.*

I pushed myself, though. I worked really, really hard. My sophomore year, I set my heart on earning the Most Improved Player award. It was my objective. My senior year, I got it.

One thing I did after each game was go over my every action during that game. Just my own. I had no control over what the other team could do. I had no control over the skill level of my teammates. I couldn't even control the position the coach put me in and how much game time I got. All I could control was me.

After I replayed the game in my head, if I felt like I did my very best in every single moment, you can bet your butt I felt like a winner. And I slept like a victorious baby.

That's the secret. When it comes right down to it, you can't control what other people around you say or do, and you didn't decide on whatever chronic illness you were assigned. All you can really control is you.

Remember that you are you, not anybody else. And today is today, not any other day. And it doesn't matter what your "best" is or isn't. All that matters is, did you do it?

How did <u>you</u>. <u>play</u>. <u>today</u>?

CHAPTER 9. WITHIN WHAT WE HAVE

Seven years ago, I spent my birthday in Ireland. People say when you go to Ireland, you need to "do it right" by taking a couple weeks or a month to travel around and see the whole country. They wait to go until they save up enough money, enough vacation days, or they retire. They wait until they have a spouse to go with or friends who are able to join in. They wait and wait and often never go. (*If you don't do it now, you're never going to do it.*)

I don't wait. But also, I didn't have the means to *do it right*. I went, yet I *did it wrong*. I was there only five days. I spent a night in Dublin and then four days in one tiny town called Carlingford, which I picked out of a book because it was within easy bus distance of Dublin and it sounded nice.

I had the most marvelous time of my life. The stories of those four days are in another book I'm writing, but suffice it to say, I had *that glow* the entire time I was there. I fell madly in love with that glorious medieval town and her jovial residents.

There are so many things we can't do. There are still more that we can't do the way everybody else can.

Stop mourning pasta and experiment with spaghetti squash. Walk the 5K you can't run anymore. Rearrange your furniture to make a special movie room in your house if the cinema has become impossible. Go to Ireland for only five days.

If you can't do it right, do it wrong.

Look away from your limitations and see what's possible to do within them and do it. Play your best.

The truth is, you may be able to do more within your limitations than you could ever do without them. That is my story....

I can attribute a single action by my friend Phil for ending my comedy career, my teaching career, and a marriage. It became so that when he greeted me, he'd never say "Hi"; he always just said, "I'm sorry."

Neither I nor he actually blamed him, of course. It was just our way at having a dark laugh at life. Phil is one of my comedian friends, and many years ago, when we happened to be booked together yet again, at a Marine bar in North Carolina, he encouraged me to call my ex-boyfriend, also a comedian.

Within barely a year, that ex and I were married. This took me to a new teaching job at a boarding school with classes running into weekends. The marriage ended because it began and never should have. Comedy ended because I fell out from my best contacts because I was no longer available on weekends. Teaching ended because the principal who came onboard my second year there turned me off of the profession maybe for good (for the record, he now has a *record.*). And because I left my job at a boarding school where I lived, I also lost my home. Talk about starting over!

Five years later, I'd gotten my feet back under me. I had the new career as an advertising copywriter, I owned my own adorable little old house, and I'd acquired no additional ex-husbands (or husbands at all). That's when I got the call from Phil. About a show.

At this point, I was pretty sure I'd fully retired from the comedy racket. I'd been onstage a mere single time in the prior four years, at a strip mall bar's ill-guided attempt at a comedy night, and I'd had no ambition to do it ever again.

But besides featuring the appealing opportunity to work with a very good friend and joke some more about how he'd ruined my life, this particular gig happened to be in my local area (though Phil had no idea I'd now lived in central Pennsylvania), and it was a fundraiser for dogs. I quickly thumbed through my vocabulary and found the word "no" to be shockingly absent.

We might say now that Phil, in making that phone call, caused my fibromyalgia.

Again, I'd been onstage once in four years, and I was about to do a show at a fancy theatre. My material was old—some of it 14 years old. I didn't relate to it anymore. I also found a good bit of it to be inappropriate for an opening act at a charity show.

I furiously went to work writing and working out material at open mic nights. An old standard for comedians is we can write and polish ten minutes of "A-level" material a year, if we really work at it. I was aiming to achieve that feat in a couple months.

Meanwhile, things were really picking up at work. I'd moved from my coordinator role into some serious copywriting, and I was buried in writing assignments while still doing my old position's work, too. Also, that was the year a third of our company either quit or got fired.

As if that wasn't enough work stress, I picked up a second job on weekends to pay for my upcoming birthday adventure to Cambodia. Instead, I ended up spending that extra income on medical tests and copays.

My grand comeback to the stage was to be November 1. By October, the mysterious illness had taken over my entire body, including my mind and my emotions. There were entire days when I was too tired to get off the couch. I had a terrifying set at an open mic where my brain just stopped and I couldn't speak. Jokes I'd done hundreds of times were suddenly erased from my tongue. I hurt, everywhere, all the time.

I was still a year away from the diagnosis, but that was it. All the stress of everything I'd taken on that fall triggered the illness I'll have for the rest of my life. I might tell Phil it's all his fault, that the stress of getting that show ready, and the time it took away from the recuperation I desperately needed, caused this disease.

Here's the rest of the story.

I made it to November 1. That night, I wasn't feeling too awful, and I was feeling pretty well prepared. Before the show, I was backstage, alone, wearing a new outfit I bought just for that night, which included some awesome overpriced black pants. I thought, this is actually going to work. I'm going to do this. I even said out loud to myself … well, I'll paraphrase … "I freakin' belong onstage."

I started cold and had them rolling by the end. I did it. I actually did it.

My proclamation and success helped trigger a plan. Only helped, because there was more to it.

I knew something was wrong, and it was something that was taking away time. My days were shorter as my moments of mental acuity were fewer. To me, time is art. Time is when I can write books and make things. Taking away my time is devastating to my soul, and that's just what this illness was doing. I recognized this loss and resolved to take the time I did have and make every moment count.

It's not unlike that brilliant new culinary invention you come up with when your fridge and cabinets are nearly empty. Or when you want to take someone out on a date, but you're broke, so you do something cool and fun that you never would have thought of if you had the scratch for dinner and a movie.

Our restrictions force a greater level of creativity.

The magic of thriving within restrictions, particularly those that seem unfair, was a lesson taught to me by comedy itself.

I was on road full time when I was 22 years old. The combination of my age and gender made me an anomaly in this world. I understood this, but never fully understood the implications until one night in Ohio when the headliner approached me after the show with an illuminating comment.

He was paying me and my show very kind compliments, but within the conversation, he said, "I usually don't watch the other comic, but you're a girl and you're young and that's so different, so I wanted to see what you could do."

That was my "wow" moment. I wondered, how many times have I been watched extra closely, scrutinized even—by the other comedians, the bookers, the managers, the random bartenders tasked with sending a report back to the booking agency—because I look different?

It was a lot, I realized. It was as if every show were an audition, and I never had the luxury of an off night or, as we say in the business, "phoning one in." I always had to be my very best, and it was always tenuous whether that was good enough. So how did I deal with this ... dare I say ... discrimination?

If every show was an audition, then I just had to treat every show like an audition, and so I did. I made sure I wrote better material, funnier. I aimed to be more commanding and present onstage. I brought the love. I focused on originality and my strength with wordplay. Plus, I did anything I could offstage to ingratiate myself. I always called ahead. I showed up early. I over-tipped the staff. I helped the other comedians sell their merchandise. I made pies.

Because I was forced to be better, guess what? I was. Had I not those unfair constraints placed upon me, I never would have had the career I've had. As a professional comedian, I've done shows in 32 states. I reached a level where I became a mentor. That inspired me to become a teacher.

The new plan which formed that November, after I returned to the stage and had the new restrictions of illness shaping my resolve, was to write a corporate comedy show and get back onstage doing the four-figure gigs instead of the three-figure gigs of my prior life's club circuit. I aimed to build up a show and a calendar so I could support myself performing, quit the corporate job, and get back all that time that I was losing. I wanted to write books.

By the time winter was in full force, I realized I wasn't feeling it. I couldn't come up with any "corporate" material that wasn't bitter and negative. I knew that wouldn't fly.

What about colleges, then?

That's when I got in touch with a friend of mine from my very beginnings in comedy. He has a company that facilitates colleges connecting with all types of artists to fill their campus activities calendars. He said, "you're a great comedian, but you should be a speaker."

I said, "Really, that's a thing? I can actually do that?"

My inner writer and those tattered remnants of my teaching life were leaping up and down in jubilation.

My first program I developed was a women's empowerment workshop. Right before I shopped my program for the first time to colleges at a conference, I got my diagnosis of fibromyalgia with chronic fatigue syndrome. It came with confirmation that this is a forever thing. I held my focus on the dream of a life onstage getting me my time back.

Also, by now, I'd had a lot of bad days and not enough days off from my day job to secretly build this side business as well as take sick days. I worked through some awful flares, promising myself that someday I'd be my own boss and could take days off when I needed to. My fibromyalgia drove me.

I developed a new program on hidden disabilities awareness. I had some personal motivation because I was frustrated with how my disability was received by some coworkers and managers. But more, it's just so very important and isn't addressed enough … yet.

I write this in the time I now have to write books, like this one. Because I did it. I built my business in those hours that remained after my days at the office, with phone calls in the parking lot on lunch breaks, and I quit that job and worked part time jobs that were physical work and hard on my body but my goal was in sight and now I'm here. I might have gotten here eventually anyway, but never so certainly and never so directly and quickly as I have because of the illness that motivates me.

Once again, my limitations are a tremendous gift that make me better than I'd ever be otherwise.

Now I have all the time back and more. Now I have so much more to say. And now I've proven to myself that I have the power to make my dreams come true, no matter what.

So when Phil and I talk lately, he begins by saying, "Hi."

CHAPTER 10. AFTER THIS

Thank you for reading all this. I hope you've felt my love for you.

Thank you for all you've already done as an advocate for us all. I hope I've inspired you to do even more, as an advocate for us, as an advocate for you, and just … *for you.*

Here's the thing about inspiration, though. Inspiration is breath, not birth. It doesn't just come once and stay like something born. It needs constant attention, like breathing. Keep seeking out inspiration. Read more books. Attend seminars. Take a class. Go to a gallery. Visit Yellowstone.

Don't just inhale inspiration. You've got to exhale it, too. Share with others what inspires you. Share your favorite ideas from this book. Share your favorite ideas about life. Be in love.

Take it in. Give it out. Steadily. In, out, in, out….

Please, keep breathing.